Amazing Snakes OF THE Southeast

Parker Holmes

PowerKiDS press
New York

Published in 2015 by The Rosen Publishing Group, Inc.
29 East 21st Street, New York, NY 10010

First Edition

Editor: Jennifer Way
Book Design: Andrew Povolny
Photo Research: Katie Stryker

Photo Credits: Cover Pete Oxford/Minden Pictures/Getty Images; p. 5 Bill Beatty/Visuals Unlimited/Getty Images; p. 6 Millard H Sharp/Photo Researchers/Getty Images; pp. 7, 12 Danita Delimont/Gallo Images/Getty Images; p. 9 John Cancalosi/PhotoLibrary/Getty Images; p. 10 Mark Newman/Lonely Planet Images/Getty Images; p. 13 James H Robinson/Photo Researchers/Getty Images; p. 15 Mark Kostich/E+/Getty Images; pp. 16, 18 George Grall/National Geographic/Getty Images; p. 19 Ed Reschke/Photo Library/Getty Images; p. 20 Joseph T Collins/Photo Researchers/Getty Images; p. 21 (top) Jack Dermid/Photo Researchers/Getty Images; p. 21(bottom) Zach Frailey/Flickr/Getty Images; p. 22 (top) Heiko Kiera/Shutterstock.com; p. 22 (middle) Rusty Dodson/Shutterstock.com; p. 22 (bottom) Jay Ondreicka/Shutterstock.com.

Library of Congress Cataloging-in-Publication Data

Holmes, Parker, author.
Amazing snakes of the Southeast / by Parker Holmes. — First edition.
pages cm. — (Amazing snakes)
Includes index.
ISBN 978-1-4777-6496-1 (library binding) — ISBN 978-1-4777-6498-5 (pbk.) — ISBN 978-1-4777-6501-2 (6-pack)
1. Snakes—Southern States—Juvenile literature. I. Title.
QL666.O6H756 2015
597.96'0975—dc23

2013044964

Manufactured in the United States of America

CPSIA Compliance Information: Batch #WS14PK6: For Further Information contact Rosen Publishing, New York, New York at 1-800-237-9932

Contents

Crawling with Snakes

If you like snakes and live in the Southeast, you're in luck! The woods and swamps here are crawling with interesting snakes. The Southeast has the warm weather and natural **habitats** that make snakes very happy. Sometimes you might even find them in your backyard. Snakes can be anywhere.

Most snakes in the Southeast won't hurt you, but a few of them can. Four types of **venomous** snakes live here: cottonmouths, rattlesnakes, copperheads, and coral snakes. These are what many people call poisonous snakes. These are the snakes you want to avoid. Their bites can be deadly! But most snakes aren't venomous. There are close to 50 **species** of nonvenomous snakes in the Southeast, along with other **subspecies**. If you see a snake here, it's most likely a harmless species, such as a garter, ribbon, racer, or water snake. Let's take a look at some exciting snakes around the Southeast.

Snakes eat their prey whole. Here, a garter snake is eating a grasshopper.

Cottonmouth

You don't want to get too close to a cottonmouth. It's one of the South's most dangerous **reptiles**. Cottonmouths have sharp fangs that **inject** venom. If they bite a person, they can do serious damage! Cottonmouths live near water, such as ponds, lakes, and swamps. That's why they're often called water moccasins.

This cottonmouth has its mouth open. You can see how it gets its name because the inside of its mouth is white.

Here, a cottonmouth is ready to strike.

These dark-colored snakes have thick bodies and typically grow to nearly 3 feet (91 cm) long. People often confuse them with nonvenomous water snakes. Cottonmouths sometimes eat harmless water snakes. Frogs and fish are other foods they like. Do you know why these snakes are called cottonmouths? The insides of their mouths are white, like the color of cotton. When they feel **threatened**, they coil up and open their mouths. If a moccasin ever shows you its mouth, watch out!

Corn Snake

Corn snakes are some of the most colorful snakes in the Southeast. They're often brightly colored in red, orange, and yellow. Corn snakes are popular pets because of their pretty colors and usually gentle behavior. They typically grow to around 4 feet (1.2 m) but can be bigger.

Corn snakes are part of the rat snake group. In fact, they're sometimes called red rat snakes. So can you guess their favorite food? That's right—rats and mice. Corn snakes kill the **rodents** by wrapping around them and squeezing. This kind of snake is called a **constrictor** because it constricts its prey.

Corn snakes have checkered patterns on their bellies that look like **maize**, or Indian corn. That may be how they got the name corn snake. Or some people say it's because the snakes are often seen around cornfields since that's where mice and rats can be found.

This corn snake is eating a mouse. Snakes eat many animals that people consider pests.

Eastern Diamondback Rattlesnake

Look at the rattles on this eastern diamondback's tail. It can shake them as a warning.

You don't want to get bitten by an eastern diamondback rattlesnake. The eastern diamondback is the largest venomous snake in the country—and possibly the most dangerous! They have thick bodies that average about 4 feet (1.2 m) long, and they sometimes grow to more than 6 feet (1.8 m). The eastern diamondback is gray or brown with dark diamond-shaped marks running down its back.

Diamondback rattlesnakes have a lot of venom to kill their prey. One of their favorite meals is rabbit. They also eat mice, rats, squirrels, and other animals. Like most snakes, diamondbacks want to be left alone. They're not looking for a fight. But if they feel threatened, they might bite. Their venom can be deadly to humans. If a rattlesnake isn't happy, it warns you by shaking the rattles on its tail. That's its way of saying, "Please go away!"

Indigo Snake

If you've ever seen an indigo snake, you're lucky. These are the largest **native** snakes in the country, and there aren't too many left. These gentle giants often grow to 6 feet (1.8 m) long and occasionally reach more than 8 feet (2.4 m)! The eastern indigo snake is found mostly in Florida and southern Georgia.

This eastern indigo snake is outside of a gopher tortoise's burrow. A burrow is an animal home made by digging into the ground.

The eastern indigo eats other snakes, even ones that are venomous! Here, one is eating a timber rattlesnake.

Indigo snakes' favorite habitats, such as longleaf pine forests, have shrunk. So they're not as common as they used to be. Indigos like to live in holes dug by gopher tortoises and armadillos. They rest in these holes and come out to hunt. They eat lizards, toads, mice, other snakes, and lots of different animals. They don't have venom, but they have powerful jaws to **subdue** prey.

Indigo snakes are solid black, but their shiny scales can have a hint of blue. That's why they're called indigo snakes. Indigo is a type of blue.

Coral Snake

Don't be fooled by the eastern coral snake. It has bright, pretty colors that make it look like a candy cane. But a bite from a coral snake can be deadly! These snakes have the most **toxic** venom of any snake in the country. The good news is that they rarely bite people. When they do, their fangs are so small that they don't usually deliver much venom. Coral snakes are shy and spend lots of time hiding. They typically grow to around 2 feet (61 cm).

Coral snakes have red, yellow, and black bands that make them look similar to several harmless snakes, such as scarlet snakes. So how do you tell them apart? On the coral snake, the red and yellow bands touch. But on harmless snakes, the red and black bands touch. Rhymes such as "Red touch yellow, kill a fellow; red touch black, friend of Jack" help people remember.

You can see the bands of color on this eastern coral snake. The pattern of colors tells you that it is a venomous snake, rather than a similar-looking nonvenomous snake.

Copperhead

It is hard to see this copperhead camouflaged among the leaves.

If you know anyone who has been bitten by a venomous snake in the Southeast, it was probably by a copperhead. Copperheads are the most common venomous snakes in this part of the country. Their bites almost never kill people, but they can be very painful.

The copperhead is closely related to the cottonmouth, or water moccasin. In fact, some people call copperheads highland moccasins. They're medium-sized snakes, usually about 2.5 feet (76 cm) long. Along with cottonmouths and rattlesnakes, they belong to the family of venomous snakes called vipers.

Even though copperheads are fairly common, they can be hard to see. That's because they have really good **camouflage**. They're light brown with darker bands and a **copper**-colored head. This coloring helps them blend in with leaves and other material in the woods. This makes it harder for **predators** to find them, and it makes it easier to **ambush** prey.

Hognose

Do you think eating a toad sounds yummy? Hognose snakes sure do. That's their favorite food. Anywhere you find toads, you might find an eastern hognose snake. These harmless snakes are found throughout the Southeast. They're medium-sized snakes, often around 2 feet (61 cm) long. They can be dark or spotted in a variety of colors. Hognose snakes are easy to identify because they have an unusual nose. It's kind of upturned and broad, like the **snout** of a hog.

Here, a hognose snake is puffing to try to scare away its enemies.

This is what a hognose looks like when it is playing dead.

When these snakes feel threatened, they put on quite a show. They'll rise up, puff out their necks kind of like the way a cobra does, open their mouths, and hiss. That's why some people call them puff adders or hissing adders. If this puffing doesn't scare away the threat, they try a new routine. They'll roll onto their backs, stick out their tongues, and play dead. Hognose snakes are very good actors!

A Great Variety

If you're looking for snakes in the Southeast, you might turn up all kinds of interesting species. If you're near water, you'll most likely find a harmless water snake. There are several different kinds here, including southern, brown, and plain-bellied, among others. If you're walking through fields or woods, you might see a black racer. Black racers are one of the fastest snakes in the country.

Garter snakes are snakes commonly found in the Southeast, as well as most of the rest of North America.

This is a black racer in North Carolina. These dark-colored snakes sometimes look a little greenish or bluish.

Or you might spot a big gray rat snake climbing a tree or maybe a king snake hiding in an old barn. Then there are all kinds of smaller snakes you might find, such as garter and ribbon snakes.

If you're scared of snakes, remember that most snakes are harmless. They're also good to have around because they eat lots of insects and rodents. The Southeast is full of many kinds of great snakes. Wouldn't you like to see one? Snakes are exciting!

The brown water snake, shown here, lives in swamps and streams throughout the Southeast.

Other Snakes in the Southeast

- Black swamp snake
- Common king snake
- Common ribbon snake
- Flat-headed snake
- Florida crowned snake
- Glossy crayfish snake
- Graham's crayfish snake
- Louisiana pine snake
- Mud snake
- Northern water snake
- Pygmy rattlesnake
- Pine snake
- Plain-bellied water snake
- Rainbow snake
- Red-bellied snake
- Rim rock crowned snake
- Rough earth snake
- Rough green snake
- Salt marsh snake
- Short-tailed snake
- Smooth earth snake
- Southeastern crowned snake
- Southern water snake
- Striped crayfish snake
- Western worm snake

Pygmy rattlesnake

Graham's crayfish snake

Salt marsh snake

Glossary

ambush (AM-bush) To attack by surprise from a hiding place.

camouflage (KA-muh-flahj) A color or a pattern that matches the surroundings and helps hide something.

constrictor (kun-STRIKT-ur) A snake that kills by wrapping its body around its prey and squeezing.

copper (KO-pur) A reddish-brown metal.

habitats (HA-buh-tats) The kinds of land where animals or plants naturally live.

inject (in-JEKT) To use a sharp object to force something into a body.

maize (MAYZ) Multicolored, starchy corn.

native (NAY-tiv) Born or grown in a certain place or country.

predators (PREH-duh-terz) Animals that kill other animals for food.

reptiles (REP-tylz) Cold-blooded animals with lungs and scales.

rodents (ROH-dents) Animals with gnawing teeth, such as mice.

snout (SNOWT) An animal's nose.

species (SPEE-sheez) A single kind of living thing. All people are one species.

subdue (sub-DOO) To bring under control.

subspecies (SUB-spee-sheez) Types within a species.

threatened (THREH-tund) Acted as though something will possibly cause hurt.

toxic (TOK-sik) Poisonous.

venomous (VEH-nuh-mis) Having a poisonous bite.

Index

Websites

Due to the changing nature of Internet links, PowerKids Press has developed an online list of websites related to the subject of this book. This site is updated regularly. Please use this link to access the list: www.powerkidslinks.com/amaz/seas/